ENS 2

Charles R. Smith Jr.

CANDLEWICK PRESS

CONTENTS

SMOOTH LIKE WHAT

A'ja game *smooth* like
chinchilla fur.
Left hand *smooth* like
the hum of a cat's purr.

Spin move *smooth* like
wind whistling on a wing.
Step-back *smooth* like
silk draped on a king.

Fadeaway *smooth* like
butter melting on biscuits.
Off-the-glass *smooth* like
the throne where a queen sits.

Jab step *smooth* like
snow untouched on a mountain.
Jump shot *smooth* like
caramel flowing from a fountain.

Dribble drive *smooth* like
a fresh donut's glaze.
Making it look easy
in so many ways,
A'ja got *smooooooth*
game for days.

A'JA WILSON

THE BAG

BREANNA STEWART

Breanna with the bag,
the **bag of tricks**,
Breanna be ballin'
to get buckets quick.

Breanna be faking
be taking
be making
off the spin
off the glass
off the hesi-
hesitation.

Breanna be ballin'
to get buckets quick,
Breanna be ballin'
with a big **bag of tricks**.

Breanna be backing
be pivoting
be flipping
hook shots
into nets
Breanna
be ripping.

Breanna be ballin'
with the **bag of tricks**,
Breanna be ballin'
to get buckets quick.

Breanna be fading
be flicking the ball in,
way out from long distance
all net
no rim.

Breanna be scoring,
scoring buckets quick,
ballin'
Breanna be
with her slick **bag of tricks**.

At **six foot nine** Brittney stands **tall**

on the court, making others look small.

With l o n g arms she swats

away opponents' shots

or scores by **dunking the ball.**

TTNEY

BRITTNEY GRINER

Chicago's Pride	**Crafty Passer**
Collects Points	**Calm Poise**
Cancels Points	**Clutch Performer**
Causes Problems	**Champion Pedigree**
Creative Playmaker	**Complete Player**
	Candace Parker

CANDACE PARKER

COURTNI

COURTNEY VANDERSLOOT

Y-VISION

See
Courtney on the court
directing the show.
See
Courtney with the ball
take charge and go.

See
Courtney with the crossover
Courtney with the no-look
Courtney with the flip pass
to the jump hook.
See
Courtney with the steal
Courtney with the bounce pass.

See
Courtney with the spinner
high off the glass.
See
Courtney with the dribble drive
Courtney go behind the back
Courtney with the shovel pass
assist at the rack.

See
Courtney off the curl.
See
Courtney catch and shoot.
Must-see CV:
see
Courtney Vandersloot!

TOO MANY GAMES

JONQUEL JONES

Jonquel Jones
with the six-six frame
growing numbers exponentially
with too many names.
J Double
with the handle,
Double J
with the J,
J Dub
with the hesi
pull-up fadeaway.
JQ
with the board,
J2
with the swat,
J Squared
with the steal
to the game-winning shot,
J Deezy
on the break
with the sick dime drop.
J Dub 3-5
anywhere behind the key,
left side
right side
knocks down the three.
Jonquel Jones
with too many names,
filling up stat sheets
with too many games.

THE UNSTO

LIZ CAMBAGE

PPABLE

Standing six foot eight
on the WNBA stage
with a globe-trotting game,
Liz Cambage.

Dominant in China,
unstoppable in Australia,
but could she be stopped
in the WNBA?

Well, one night in Dallas
Liz let them know
what a **force** she could be
when she put on a show.

2 points from the left side pull-up
2 from the right wing mid-range
2 from the left side post-up
3 from the top left
2 from the roll to the rim
2 from the left wing
2 from the spin move to the rim
2 from the top left
2 from the paint post-up off the glass
2 from the right side post-up
2 from the left side drive
3 from the top of the key
2 from the right elbow
2 from the post layup
2 from the left side post-up off the glass
2 off the right side dribble drive
3 from the top of the key
plus **15** free throws
for a record-breaking **53,**
the most points in one game
in WNBA history.
An **unstoppable** force
on the WNBA stage
conquering the world,
Liz Cambage!

SCORING MACHINE

DIANA TAURASI

Power up
start her up
DT3,
Scoring Machine
Diana Taurasi.
Featuring
quick feet and
versatility,
able to score
any way
instantly.
Spin moves
step-backs
feathery finger rolls
reverse layups
and Euro-step strolls
all rack up points,
points for **DT,**
but wait,
there's more:
DT shoots the three.

That's right:
the Scoring Machine
shoots the three
with pinpoint precision
and accuracy.
Off one foot or two
off-balance
off the glass
off the screen
off the dribble
off the catch-and-shoot pass,
and as an added bonus
DT can pass.

Behind the back
no-look
or skip across the floor,
DT racks up assists,
adding to the score.

But wait,
there's still more:

**Scoring Machine
DT3
is powered by heart
and competitive fury
and when the game
is on the line,
Clutch Mode is engaged
locking eyes on the twine.**

**Confidence builds,
wrist flicks the ball
toward the rim
before it falls
through the net
for victory,
thanks to
the Scoring Machine
DT3!**

DOIN'

ELENA DELLE DONNE

Elena Delle Donne
doing her thing,
Delle Donne doin' it
on the right and left wing.

Dribble
stop
spin
pop
wrist
flick
ball
drop.
Shake
bake
pump fake
step
back
elevate.
Squared
up
outside the key
catch
step
easy three.

Delle Donne doin' it
doing her thing,
Delle Donne on the blocks
doin' work for her team.

Post up
   hand up
      catch
         spin
            to the cup.
            Fake right
            shoot left
            fadeaway
            into the net.
         Step in
      step back
      step through
      to the rack.

Delle Donne doin' it
   doing her thing,
      Delle Donne dancing
         to make the nets sing!

THE OGWUM SISTER

NNEKA OGWUMIKE

Nigeria
Stanford
mother is great
block party
and 1

IKE
S

CHINEY OGWUMIKE

middle Child
six three
God gives
number one
relentless
rookie of the year

21

S-S-S-S

Southpaw
Skylar
sly
skittery
slithery
snaking
sneaking
slippery
sidewinding
smoothly
shifting
swiftly
skating
slicing
scoring
skillfully
Southpaw
Skylar
shoulders
shimmying

KYLAR

SKYLAR DIGGINS-SMITH

SUE BIRD

Smooth
Unafraid
Effortless

Basketball
IQ
Ravages
Defenses

POEM NOTES

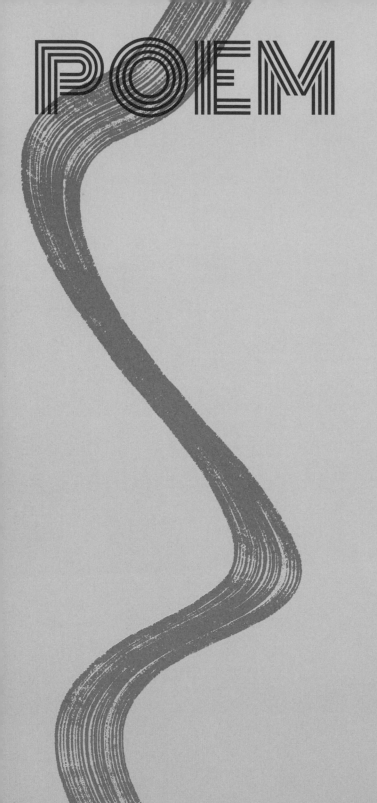

A'JA WILSON
Smooth Like What

Whenever I watch A'ja Wilson play, the word that always pops up is *smooth*. She makes everything look easy, so in my poem about her, I compared her game to things that are smooth. I started with the smoothest fur, chinchilla. Then I thought about other things that are associated with being smooth and created a variety of similes based on different parts of her game.

BREANNA STEWART
The Bag

In basketball, if you have a lot of moves you can call on to get your shot, you're known to have a "bag," as in a "bag of tricks." Not only does Breanna Stewart have a bag; she has a deep bag filled with endless tricks. For her poem, I broke down her moves one by one and then used as few words as possible to describe them. Since her name starts with a *B*, I wanted to use the verb *be* and add *ballin'* to make a play on words, saying "Breanna be ballin'," which also sounds like "Breanna b-ballin'."

BRITTNEY GRINER
A Limerick for Brittney

As one of the tallest players in the WNBA, Brittney Griner makes the game look easy. With her long arms, she swats away shots and catches passes that her defenders can't reach. But not only is Brittney tall; she is also athletic, able to run fast and jump well. She often uses her combination of skills to nab a rebound, dribble downcourt, and finish with a dunk, which not many WNBA players can do. I decided to do a limerick for her because it packs a lot of info into a few simple lines.

CANDACE PARKER
CP

During a game in which Candace Parker was playing, a commentator mentioned how well "CP" was performing. I ran with that for her poem, deciding to use only words that started with those two letters. The key, however, was choosing word pairings that would show everything she can do, and do with style. Candace is from Chicago, so I acknowledge that first with "Chicago's Pride." And not only does she score with the best in the league, but she is also a tremendous shot blocker, so I used the phrase "Cancels Points." And since she has won so many awards at every level, I also wanted to acknowledge her "Champion Pedigree."

COURTNEY VANDERSLOOT
Courtney-vision

Like a movie director, a good point guard can see things others can't and make things happen as they want them to. A good director also knows how to get everyone involved so they can all contribute. Courtney Vandersloot plays this role with ease. To follow that idea, I imagined her as a director, calling "action" and making spectacular plays by passing the ball and getting contributions from everyone. I end with a play on the phrase "must-see TV" with "Must-see CV," using Courtney's initials.

JONQUEL JONES
Too Many Games

Jonquel Jones has a skill set that doesn't match up with her height. She stands tall, at six foot six, but she can pass and get steals like a point guard. She can shoot the three like a shooting guard. She can block shots like a center. And she can rebound, post up, and score like a forward. All that adds up to a full stat sheet. Anytime I hear a name that has the same first and last initials, I try to use that when I write about them, so in her poem, I give each of her separate "games" a nickname based on her initials.

LIZ CAMBAGE
The Unstoppable
Liz Cambage's story is a bit different from that of many other players because she didn't play in college. She's from Australia and played in China and other parts of the world. At six foot six, she dominated on her Australian team and everywhere else she played. But the question was, Could she do it in the WNBA? She answered that question by scoring the most points in a game in WNBA history (at this time of writing), so in my poem about her, I detail each point she scored in that game in the order she scored them.

DIANA TAURASI
Scoring Machine
Watching Diana Taurasi play is like watching a machine. If the ball is in her hands, you know that when she shoots it, it's going in. She also has great passing ability and can play well in the clutch, so I decided to take on the voice of an infomercial host to show all the ways she can score and contribute. It was fun to write her poem like an infomercial, using phrases like, "but wait, there's more," to show off all her skills.

ELENA DELLE DONNE
Doin' It
I love the way Elena Delle Donne's last name sounds when repeated, so I created a chorus, or refrain, like in a song, based around that. Since her game is well rounded, I used simple action verbs to create a nice rhythm and show her skill set.

NNEKA OGWUMIKE AND CHINEY OGWUMIKE
The Ogwumike Sisters
Nneka and Chiney Ogwumike have beautiful names—I decided to do an acrostic of their names to talk about their individual and shared traits. They have been lucky enough to play together since they were kids. They both went to Stanford University, were both drafted number one, and both play hard on the court. Nneka, the older sister by two years, blocks shots as easily as she makes them, and Chiney can do the same. At six foot two, Nneka plays forward and has a knack for getting fouled as she shoots to get the additional point ("and 1" in the poem) with a free throw. Chiney is six three; she plays forward and center and is relentless on the boards when fighting for rebounds. Their parents are Nigerian; Nneka's name means "mother is great" in the Igbo language, while Chiney's name means "God gives."

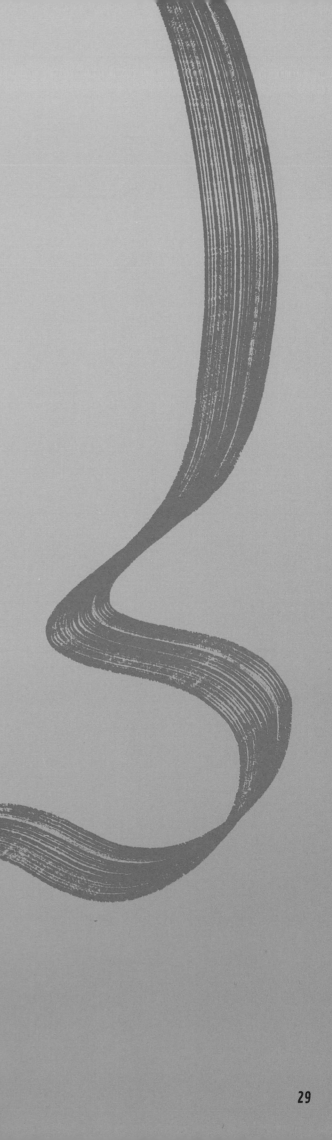

SKYLAR DIGGINS-SMITH
S-S-S-Skylar

It's always fun to watch a southpaw, or lefty, play since they do things a little bit differently. Since Skylar's name starts with an *S*, I used only words that start with *S* to describe her game.

SUE BIRD

Given Sue Bird's last name, I knew I wanted to do an acrostic using it. But as I settled on the best four words to describe her, I felt I needed more. So I added her first name to paint a clearer picture of how she makes the game look so easy.

Dedicated to Jan, my feisty teammate in life

Text copyright © 2024 by Charles R. Smith Jr.

Photography Credits

pp. 2–3: copyright © 2022 by Erica Denhoff/Icon Sportswire

pp. 4–5: copyright © 2021 by AP Photo/John Locher

pp. 6–7: copyright © 2021 by AP Photo/Chase Stevens

p. 9: copyright © 2022 by Erica Denhoff/Icon Sportswire

pp. 10–11: copyright © 2020 by AP Photo/Phelan M. Ebenhack

pp. 12–13: copyright © 2021 by Sean D. Elliot/The Day via AP

pp. 14–15: copyright © 2012 by AP Photo/Sergio Perez, Pool

p. 17: copyright © 2020 by AP Photo/Chris O'Meara

pp. 18–19: copyright © 2018 by Ron Waite/CSM

p. 20: copyright © 2019 by Jevone Moore/Icon Sportswire

p. 21: copyright © 2019 by M. Anthony Nesmith/Icon Sportswire

pp. 22–23: copyright © 2017 by AP Photo/Tony Gutierrez

pp. 24–25: copyright © 2018 by AP Photo/Elaine Thompson

First edition 2024

Library of Congress Catalog Card Number pending
ISBN 978-1-5362-2534-1

24 25 26 27 28 29 CCP 10 9 8 7 6 5 4 3 2 1

Printed in Shenzhen, Guangdong, China

This book was typeset in Contrail One.
Digital artwork and typography by Lauren Pettapiece and Tif Bucknor.

Candlewick Press
99 Dover Street
Somerville, Massachusetts 02144

www.candlewick.com

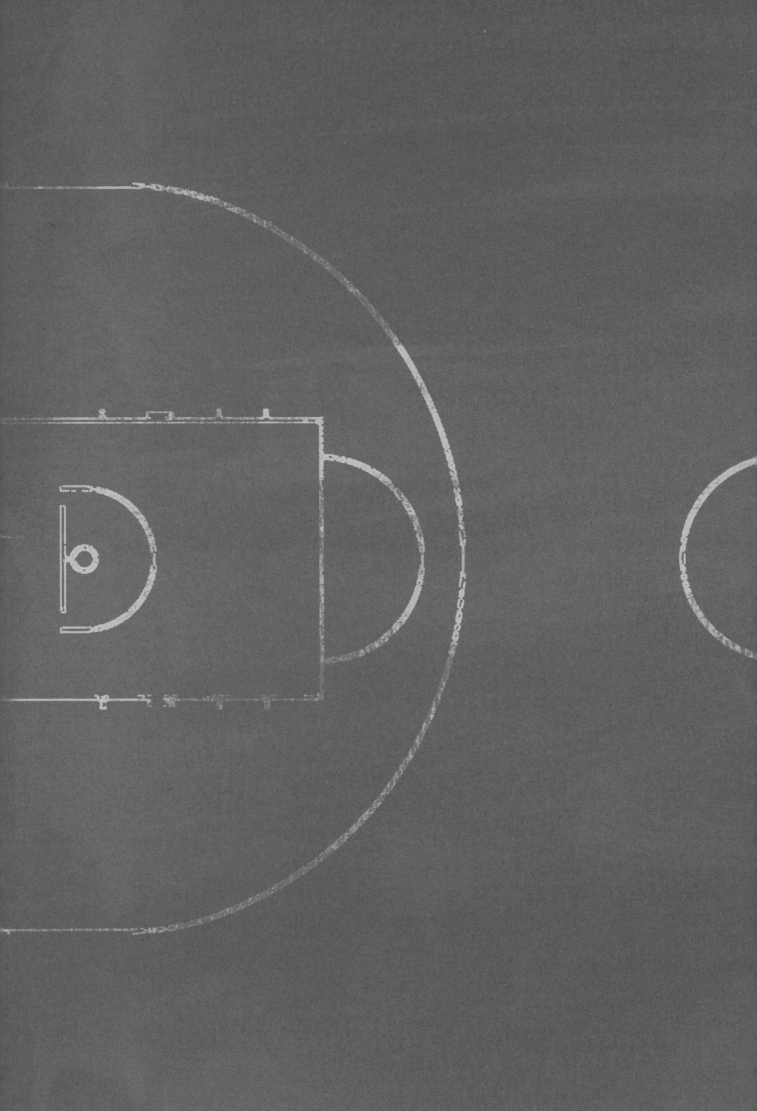